Kim Diehl
Simple Appliqué

Approachable Techniques • Easy Methods • Beautiful Results!

Martingale
Create with Confidence

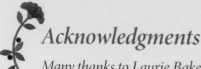

Acknowledgments

Many thanks to Laurie Baker for traveling down this how-to-appliqué road with me. As always, your knowledge, guidance, and expertise (along with your endless good humor and wicked wit) made the journey a complete pleasure.

My appreciation to the staff at the Gathering Place in Rupert, Idaho, for machine-quilting "Scrap Basket Blossoms" so beautifully.

A huge thank-you to everyone in the Martingale office who had a hand in helping me share my favorite appliqué techniques, tips, and tricks, with special thanks to Brent Kane for your spot-on photography skills—if a picture is worth a thousand words, then this book truly contains a wealth of knowledge.

Simple Appliqué: Approachable Techniques, Easy Methods, Beautiful Results!

© 2015 by Kim Diehl

Martingale®
19021 120th Ave. NE, Ste. 102
Bothell, WA 98011-9511 USA
ShopMartingale.com

Printed in China
20 19 18 17 16 15   8 7 6 5 4 3 2 1

**Library of Congress Cataloging-in-Publication Data
is available upon request.**

ISBN: 978-1-60468-627-2

MISSION STATEMENT

Dedicated to providing quality products and service to inspire creativity.

CREDITS

PUBLISHER AND CHIEF VISIONARY OFFICER
Jennifer Erbe Keltner

EDITORIAL DIRECTOR
Karen Costello Soltys

ACQUISITIONS EDITOR
Karen M. Burns

TECHNICAL EDITOR
Laurie Baker

COPY EDITOR
Sheila Chapman Ryan

DESIGN DIRECTOR
Paula Schlosser

PHOTOGRAPHER
Brent Kane

PRODUCTION MANAGER
Regina Girard

INTERIOR DESIGNERS
Regina Girard and
Connor Chin

ILLUSTRATOR
Christine Erikson

Contents

Introduction 5

Preparing to Appliqué 6

Invisible Machine Appliqué 8

Invisible Machine Appliqué
  with Trapunto 30

Needle-Turn Appliqué 32

Fusion Appliqué 38

Wool Appliqué 41

Fusible Appliqué 50

Practice Project:
  Scrap Basket Blossoms 53

About the Author 63

 Introduction

It's no secret that I love quilts. And quilts with appliqué? Even better!

After many years of attending quilt-guild meetings all around the country, teaching numerous workshops, and meeting scads of quiltmakers, I've learned that people often have really strong feelings about appliqué. Some are completely in love with it, and some . . . not so much. I'll be the first to admit that appliqué can seem intimidating, but like most things, when it's broken down into simple, doable steps, it's very approachable and can be a snap. Honest!

I've always felt that one of the most appealing aspects about the art of quiltmaking, and appliqué specifically, is that it's not a "one-size-fits-all" craft. Because quilts are made by a variety of people for a wide range of uses, there are countless ways to accomplish the individual steps from start to finish.

Being a self-taught quiltmaker has enabled me to approach my appliqué techniques without having any preconceived notions about what I should (or shouldn't) do, and I've experimented for years with various types of appliqué to find the simplest and most efficient methods to suit any type of quilt while also producing beautiful results. What's really great about all of this experimentation is that it's enabled me to weed out the steps that are less than stellar and focus on what really works.

The techniques shared in this book have been fine-tuned and tweaked through the years, and I find myself turning to them again and again as I make my own quilts. To sweeten the pot, I've included many little tips and tricks to make the journey even smoother as you explore these methods. With an adventurous spirit, a deep breath, and a little practice, you'll find that appliqué can be easy to include in your quilts!

Kim

Preparing to Appliqué

After stitching dozens and dozens (and dozens!) of quilts through the years, I've learned that taking a moment for a couple of quick preparation steps at the start of a new appliqué project helps to streamline the process and enables me to spend my time more efficiently. The information that follows explains the benefit of adding creased registration marks for easy design layout, and I've shared a quick tip for protecting the edges of your appliqué blocks to prevent fraying.

Protecting Block Edges

I've found that some fabrics withstand being handled through the appliqué process very well, while others ravel with very little use. If you feel that fraying may occur as you work on your project, take a moment to stabilize the block edges and protect the seam allowances.

I recommend using a product called Fray Check, which is a little bit like thin, clear nail polish. When applied to the edges of your fabric, Fray Check will stiffen them slightly to prevent the threads from raveling. Incorporating this step will eliminate the need to cut your block backgrounds larger than needed, and then trim them down to size after the appliqué process is complete. To easily apply Fray Check, here's a great little technique I use.

1. Place the fabric on a tabletop, with the edge of the cloth extending just beyond the table edge closest to you.

2. Hold the bottle of Fray Check in your dominant hand and rest your other hand against the side edge of the table, below the extending cloth edge. Steady your hand holding the bottle on top of the hand resting against the table and touch the tip of the bottle to the edge of the cloth to begin the flow. Slide your bottom hand along the table edge to apply a thin line of Fray Check to the cloth, rotating the piece and repeating the process to protect each side **(fig. 1)**. Let dry.

"Blackbirds and Berries," from Homestyle Quilts, *coauthored with Laurie Baker*

Fig. 1 Move the bottom hand while it supports the hand holding the bottle.

Evaluating Your Design and Pressing Registration Marks

As you begin each new appliqué project, take a moment to evaluate how the design is positioned on the block or unit to be stitched. Very often, you'll see designs centered, whether from side to side, top to bottom, or diagonally, but occasionally you'll have a design that requires measuring from a given point or simply placing the elements to create a visually pleasing design. Before you lay out your design, pressing creases into the cloth will act as registration marks to simplify the process of positioning your appliqués.

When adding creases to serve as registration marks for a block background or unit, it's best to press the creases using a hot, dry iron (I usually use the cotton setting). Using steam can make creases difficult to "un-press" after the stitching is complete.

Pressing the fabric with right sides together will produce inverted creases, making it much easier to position and stitch the appliqués, as opposed to folding the fabric with wrong sides together, which will produce raised creases with peaked centers.

To add a perfectly centered crease (in any direction needed), fold the background fabric in half to find the center position, aligning the raw edges to ensure the piece remains square, and use the heated iron to press the resulting center crease.

Crease Styles

I've found that for nearly all appliqué projects, adding one or more of the creases described below can be tremendously beneficial when laying out the design.

Vertical design. If the majority of your design is based on a center vertical position, crease the block through the vertical center **(fig. 1)**.

Horizontal design. For designs that are based on a horizontal position, crease the block through the horizontal center **(fig. 2)**.

Vertical and horizontal design. For designs that feature both vertically and horizontally centered elements, crease the block through both the horizontal and vertical centers, refolding the cloth as each crease is added **(fig. 3)**.

Diagonal design. If the project features a diagonal design, fold the cloth in half diagonally and crease the fold, and then unfold and refold the cloth in the opposite diagonal direction to add the second crease **(fig. 4)**.

Combination. For designs that include all of the above elements, press horizontal, vertical, and diagonal creases, unfolding and refolding to add each new crease **(fig. 5)**.

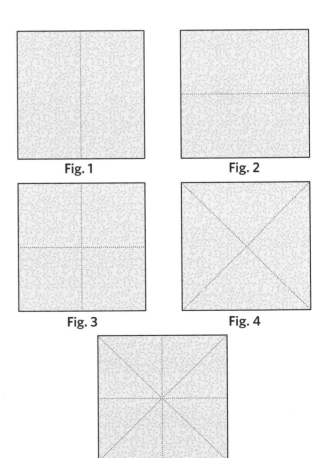

Fig. 1

Fig. 2

Fig. 3

Fig. 4

Fig. 5

7

Invisible Machine Appliqué

My invisible-machine-appliqué technique uses freezer paper to form the shapes for stitching and produces results that closely resemble hand-stitched needle-turn appliqué, but it's infinitely quicker to complete. Among its many benefits are shortened stitching time, finished appliqués that aren't reversed from the original pattern (as often happens with freezer-paper techniques), and preparation that eliminates the need to anchor seam allowances in place with starch or a fabric glue stick prior to stitching. This is hands down my favorite technique when I want stitched appliqués with turned-under edges for a beautifully finished look.

Materials

In addition to standard quiltmaking supplies, the following tools and products are needed for this method:

- .004 monofilament thread in smoke and clear colors
- Awl or stiletto with a *sharp* point
- Bias bars in various widths (for designs featuring stems and vines)
- Embroidery scissors with a fine, sharp point
- Freezer paper
- Iron with a sharp pressing point (travel-sized or mini appliqué irons work well for this technique)
- Liquid fabric glue, water-soluble and acid-free (my favorite brand is Quilter's Choice by Beacon Adhesives)
- Glue stick for fabric, water-soluble and acid-free
- Open-toe presser foot
- Pressing board with a *firm* surface
- Sewing machine with adjustable tension control, capable of producing a tiny zigzag stitch
- Size 75/11 (or smaller) machine-quilting needles
- Tweezers with rounded tips

"Four and Twenty Blackbirds," from Simple Charm

Preparing Pattern Tracing Templates

For projects featuring multiple appliqués made from a single pattern (for example, more than a dozen of the same leaf or flower), I've found that being able to trace around a sturdy template to make the pieces needed, rather than tracing shapes from the pattern sheet numerous times, speeds up the process tremendously and gives consistent results. Simply trace around the template onto freezer paper as many times as needed. The resulting shapes will be the same and it's much quicker than repeatedly tracing the shape from the book.

Any time a template is used, only one will be needed; it's simply a tracing tool to enable you to easily make the individual freezer-paper pattern pieces you'll use when preparing the appliqués from fabric. To make a sturdy paper template for tracing your pattern pieces (which eliminates the need to buy template plastic), use the steps that follow:

1. Cut a single piece of freezer paper about twice as large as your shape. Use a pencil to trace the pattern onto one end of the non-waxy side of the paper **(fig. 1)**.

2. Fold the freezer paper in half, waxy sides together, and use a hot, dry iron (I turn mine to the cotton setting) to fuse the folded paper layers together **(fig. 2)**.

• PIN POINT •

Two-Step Pressing Process

For templates that will stand up to repeated use, I first press the freezer-paper layers from the front of the shape, and then turn the layered unit over and finish pressing it from the back. Pressing the layers in two steps will remove any ripples or air bubbles and result in shapes that are super-sturdy and easy to trace around.

3. Cut out the shape exactly on the drawn line, taking care to duplicate it accurately **(fig. 3)**.

Fig. 1 Trace the pattern from the book onto the dull side of the freezer paper.

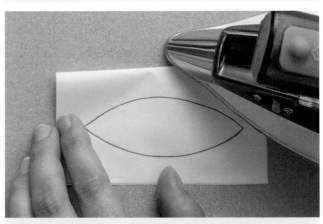

Fig. 2 Press the freezer paper layers together.

Fig. 3 Cut out the freezer-paper template.

Preparing Paper Pattern Pieces

Pattern *pieces* are used differently than pattern *templates;* pieces are individual freezer-paper shapes that you'll use to prepare your appliqués from fabric. Always cut your paper pattern pieces on the drawn lines, because you'll add the seam allowances later when you cut the shapes from your fabrics. To achieve smooth pattern edges, I suggest moving the paper, rather than the scissors, as you take long, smooth cutting strokes.

Use the prepared template (or printed pattern, if you're preparing fewer than a dozen pieces) to trace the specified number of pattern pieces onto the non-waxy side of a piece of freezer paper **(fig. 4)**.

Stacked Layers

To save time when many appliqué pieces are required from any given symmetrical shape, trace the pattern onto the non-waxy side of a piece of freezer paper as previously instructed. Stack additional freezer-paper pieces underneath the traced paper (up to eight layers for simple shapes, and four to six layers for more curvy or complex shapes) with the waxy sides all facing down. Anchor the layers together using a pin in the center of the shape to prevent shifting, or use staples at regular intervals slightly *outside* the shape in the background area. (For larger appliqués, I place a single pin in the center of the shape to prevent shifting and also staple the background areas.) Cut out the pattern pieces exactly on the drawn lines of the top piece of freezer paper and discard the background areas **(fig. 5)**.

Fig. 4 Use the template to trace the pattern shapes onto freezer paper.

• PIN POINT •

Achieving Smooth Edges

When cutting freezer-paper pattern pieces, I find that it's not as important to cut the shapes precisely on the drawn lines as it is to achieve smoothly flowing edges. Remember that the pattern pieces being cut at this stage will form the shapes that are ultimately stitched onto your quilt top, so any imperfections should be trimmed away and fine-tuned. After cutting, I always turn the pinned stack of pattern pieces to the back to enable me to better evaluate the shape and smooth away any cutting flaws without having the distraction of the drawn lines.

Fig. 5 Layer freezer paper pieces to cut multiple symmetrical shapes.

Accordion Folding

For shapes without an obvious direction, even if they're not perfectly symmetrical, I use an accordion-fold technique to quickly make multiple pattern pieces. To do this, trace the shape onto one end of the non-waxy side of a strip of freezer paper as previously instructed, and then fold the strip accordion-style (up to eight layers deep) in widths to fit your shape **(fig. 6)**. Anchor the layers together as previously instructed, cut out the pattern pieces exactly on the drawn lines of the top layer, and discard the background areas.

To prepare mirror-image or reversed pattern pieces for shapes with an obvious direction (such as a bird), use the accordion-fold technique described above to trace and cut out the shape. After cutting and separating the layers, every other shape will be a mirror image **(fig. 7)**.

Fig. 6 For pieces that have no obvious direction, cut multiple pattern pieces from an accordion-folded strip of freezer paper.

• PIN POINT •

Mixing Regular and Reversed Shapes

As a matter of personal preference, I use the accordion-fold technique for all pattern shapes that aren't obviously directional, such as leaves and flowers. Randomly using a mix of the regular and reversed shapes brings a subtle element of interest to my appliqué designs for added appeal.

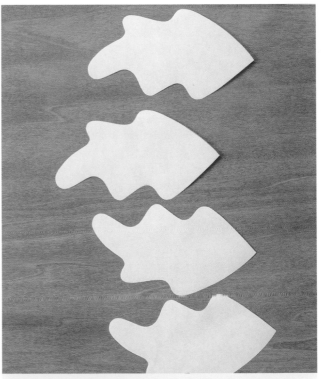

Fig. 7 Use the accordion-fold technique to create mirror-image shapes.

"Bittersweet Briar," from Simple Graces

Preparing the Appliqués

1. Apply a small amount of glue from a fabric glue stick to the center of the dull side of each paper pattern piece (for larger shapes, apply several small areas of glue, keeping the glue in the center of the shape and away from the edges where the appliqués will be stitched). Affix the prepared freezer-paper pattern pieces to the *wrong* side of your fabrics *with the shiny, waxy sides up,* leaving approximately ½" between each shape for seam allowances. Experience has taught me that positioning the longest lines or curves of each shape on the diagonal is best, because the resulting bias edges are easier to work with than straight-grain edges when pressing the seam allowances onto the paper pattern pieces to prepare them for stitching **(fig. 8).** Of course, pattern pieces can be positioned in any way that pleases you to take advantage of directional prints or stripes, but this is the rule of thumb I follow.

2. Using embroidery scissors (my tool of choice because the smaller size gives more control when cutting curvy or smaller-scale appliqués), cut out each shape, adding an approximate ¼" seam allowance around the paper **(fig. 9).**

Fig. 8 Position pattern pieces with the longest line on the bias of the fabric, shiny sides up.

Fig. 9 Add a seam allowance when cutting out the fabric shape.

• PIN POINT •

Previewing the Pattern Piece Placement on the Fabric

When working with large-scale prints or prints you'd like to "fussy cut" (this means that you choose the placement of the print on the shape, rather than positioning it randomly), you can audition the placement of the appliqué on the fabric before you cut out the shape. To do this, affix the pattern piece to the fabric with a glue stick, and then hold it up to a window or under a ceiling light with the right side of the fabric facing you to view the pattern-piece placement. If you're less than pleased, remove the pattern piece and reposition it (applying more glue if needed). This little trick is like using a light box, and it gives you the opportunity to preview your finished appliqué for perfect print placement.

"Short and Sweet," from Simple Charm

3. After the seam allowances have been added, clip all inner points and any pronounced inner curves. Use embroidery scissors to make one clip at the center of the curve, directing it straight toward the pattern piece and stopping two or three threads away from the paper edge **(fig. 10).** Stopping a couple of threads away from the paper will give you a small intact edge of fabric to wrap over the side of the appliqué pattern piece, while the clip in the seam allowance will enable the fabric to conform to the shape. If you're unsure whether an inner curve is pronounced enough to need a clip, try pressing it without one (as described in "Pressing Appliqués" on page 14); if the fabric easily follows the shape of the curve and lies flat, you've eliminated a step! Leave outer curves unclipped, as this will reduce fraying and make the seam allowances easier to work with.

Fig. 10 Clip inner points and curves at the center or deepest part of the point or curve.

• PIN POINT •

Cutting the Perfect Seam Allowance

For my invisible-machine-appliqué technique, I've learned that when it comes to seam allowances, more is definitely more. Cutting your seam allowances too narrowly can make the fabric more difficult to handle and increase the possibility of fraying. With that being said, cutting the seam allowances too wide can also make it challenging to position them on the back of the shape and achieve smoothly finished edges. A great little trick to help you gauge the proper seam-allowance width as you prepare your shapes is to apply a strip of quilter's ¼" tape to the thumbnail of your hand that will be holding the appliqué as you cut the shape from fabric. This strip of tape provides a great visual guide for adding the perfect amount of seam allowance. As you become more proficient, you'll instinctively know the right amount to add without needing the tape.

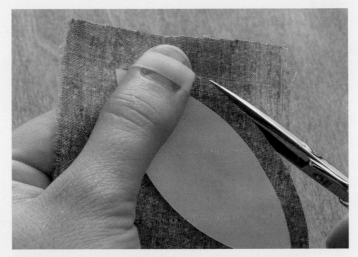

Quilter's ¼" tape provides a visual guide for cutting the perfect seam-allowance width.

Pressing Appliqués

For my invisible-machine-appliqué technique, I press appliqué seam allowances onto the waxy side of the freezer-paper pattern pieces using a hot, dry iron, rather than anchoring them in place for stitching using starch or fabric glue stick as is often done with other techniques. This approach makes it easy to remove the paper pattern pieces without the need to loosen the glued areas by spraying them with water.

It's important to use an ironing board with a *firm* surface, because this will simplify the pressing step and help you achieve beautifully prepared shapes. Pressing boards with a soft, spongy surface make it more difficult to position and press the seam allowances, because the pad shifts underneath the appliqués while you work with them.

1. Set your iron to the cotton setting and turn off the steam feature. Lay the appliqué on the pressing surface with the waxy side of the pattern piece facing up. Beginning along a gentle curve or a straight area, with that edge of the shape on the side farthest away from you, smooth the seam allowance onto the pattern piece using your index finger. Sweep the point of the iron onto the seam allowance as you slide your finger away, using downward pressure with the iron to adhere the fabric to the waxy surface of the pattern piece **(fig. 11)**.

2. If you're right-handed, continue working in small increments by rotating the appliqué clockwise toward the iron; if you're left-handed, simply reverse the direction as you work around the shape.

As you press, continue smoothing the seam allowance onto the pattern piece with your finger, drawing the seam allowance slightly back toward the previous pressed area and using the point of the iron to anchor it in place **(fig. 12)**. The curvier the shape, the smaller the increments should be as you press. Small increments enable the fabric to hug the curves of the appliqué for flawless results.

Fig. 11 Smooth the seam allowance onto the waxy side of the paper pattern piece with your finger, followed by the point of the iron.

Fig. 12 Continue around the shape, smoothing and pressing the seam allowance onto the pattern piece.

• PIN POINT •

Holding Power

I routinely let the point of my iron rest on each newly pressed section of seam allowance, holding it in place with a bit of pressure as I draw the next section over onto the paper pattern piece with my finger. I've learned that allowing the iron to rest in place while each new seam-allowance section is positioned will lengthen the amount of time the fabric receives heat, and this will help the cloth fuse more firmly to the paper pattern piece.

3. To achieve sharp outer points, press the seam allowances so the folded edge of the fabric extends beyond the first side of the pattern point, snugging the fabric firmly up against the paper edge **(fig. 13).** Fold over the seam allowance on the remaining side of the point and continue pressing the shape **(fig. 14).**

4. Because fabric won't stick to fabric without some help, after the seam allowance of the entire appliqué has been pressed, apply a small amount of fabric glue stick to the bottom of the folded flap of fabric seam allowance at the point. If the seam-allowance flap will be visible from the front of the appliqué, use the point of an awl or stiletto to drag the fabric in and away from the appliqué edge (not down from the point, as this will blunt it), and press it with the point of a hot iron to heat set the glue and fuse it in place. For narrow points, I like to roll the seam allowances under slightly as I draw them in from the edge of the shape with the awl **(fig. 15);** this will enable the seams to be completely hidden from the front of the appliqué and help them fit onto the back of the point.

5. To prepare an inner point or curve, stop pressing the seam allowance just before the center clipped section. Reaching under the appliqué at the clip, use the pad of

Fig. 13 Press the seam allowance so the fold extends beyond the pattern point.

Fig. 14 Fold over the seam allowance on the remaining side of the point.

Fig. 15 Draw the seam allowance at the point away from the appliqué edge.

• PIN POINT •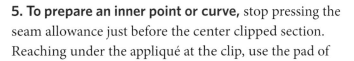

Making Sharp Points

To make the beautiful, sharp appliqué points we all strive for, ensure that your pressed seam allowance follows the line of the curve at the point, rather than flaring out from the point. I've often found that when a point is less than perfect, it's because the seam allowance isn't hugging the paper pattern piece. Following the angle of the curve leading up to each point as you press will ensure the cloth hugs the pattern piece, and the finished point will be crisp and precise.

Wrong   Correct!

your index finger to smooth the fabric leading up to the clipped position snugly onto the paper. Follow with the iron in a sweeping motion to fuse the fibers into place on the paper **(fig 16)**. Smooth the fabric on the unpressed side of the clipped seam allowance onto the paper and continue pressing **(fig. 17)**.

6. For narrow inner points or really pronounced inner curves, follow step 4 using the point of an awl or a stiletto (instead of your finger) to help grab and position the seam allowance for pressing, snugging the fabric well against the pattern piece **(fig. 18)**.

7. Turn your prepared appliqué over to the front to evaluate your pressing and adjust any areas that could be improved. Tiny imperfections can often be smoothed away by nudging them with the point of your hot iron. More pronounced imperfections are generally the result of a pleat that has formed along the seam allowance on the wrong side of the appliqué; any pleat can be loosened and re-pressed from the back, spreading and smoothing it out to remove the imperfection **(fig. 19)**.

Fig. 16 Use your finger to smooth the seam allowance on one side of the clip onto the pattern piece, and then press in place.

Fig. 17 Smooth the seam allowance on the remaining side of the clip onto the pattern piece and press in place.

• PIN POINT •

Taking up the Excess Fabric

Don't worry if there are pleats in the seam allowances on the wrong side of your appliqués after preparing and pressing them. Small pleats and gathers help take up the excess fabric, enabling the seam allowance to fit onto the back of the shape. I've learned to think of these areas like I do the gathered fabric at the center of a yo-yo—pleats along the inner seam-allowance edge are fine as long as they fan out and become smooth at the outer edge of the shape, resulting in a smooth look from the front.

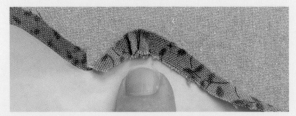

Pleats in the seam allowance are fine as long as they smooth out at the appliqué edge.

Fig. 18 Use an awl to position the seam allowance of pronounced inner points and curves.

Fig. 19 Loosen pleat from pattern and re-press.

Cutting Bias Strips

In order to make bias-tube stems and vines, you'll first need to cut bias strips. The steps provided below are my preferred method for cutting these strips. You'll end up with a manageable size of cloth that produces strips approximately twice the cut length once they're unfolded. Another benefit of this method is that you can join the cut strips end to end to make one long length, and then cut the exact pieces you need from this joined strip, resulting in little or no waste.

1. After pressing the fabric smooth, lay it in a single layer on a large cutting mat. Grasp one corner of the fabric and fold it back to form a layered triangle of any size you choose, aligning the top straight edge with the straight grain of the bottom layer of fabric **(fig 20).**

2. Rotate the layered piece of cloth to align the folded edge with a cutting line on your mat, ensuring the fold is resting evenly along the marked line to prevent a "dog-leg" curve in your strips after they've been cut and unfolded.

3. Use an acrylic ruler and rotary cutter to cut through the folded edge of cloth a few inches in from one pointed end. Begin cutting strips at measured intervals from this edge using the dimensions called for in your pattern instructions **(fig. 21).** If you reach the end of the folded edge of cloth and require additional strips, simply begin again at step 1 and repeat the process, using another corner of your cloth or squaring up the end from which you've been cutting.

4. Square off the strip ends (fig. 22) and trim them to the desired length, or sew multiple squared-off lengths together to achieve one long strip, enabling the individual lengths needed to be cut from this joined strip with minimal waste. Press the seam allowances of any joined strips to one side, not open, all in the same direction.

Fig. 20 Fold the fabric corner back to form a layered triangle.

Fig. 21 Make the first cut a few inches from one pointed end and then measure in from this edge to make additional cuts.

Fig. 22 Square off the strip ends.

Making Bias-Tube Stems and Vines

To prepare finished stems and vines that can be curved flawlessly and don't require the seam allowances to be turned under, I use bias-cut fabric strips in combination with bias bars. Using bias strips simplifies the steps needed to press and prepare the sewn tubes for stitching. After cutting the bias strips as specified on page 17, prepare them as follows:

1. With *wrong* sides together (you should be looking at the "pretty" side of the print as you work with it), fold the strip in half lengthwise and stitch a scant ¼" from the long raw edges to form a tube **(fig. 23).** I stitch my seams a few threads less than a true ¼", as this often eliminates the need to trim the seam allowance and allows the bias bar to slide through the sewn fabric tube more easily.

2. For any stem sewn from a strip 1"-wide or less, you'll likely need to trim the seam allowances a tiny bit so they'll be hidden when the stem is viewed from the front **(fig. 24).**

3. Insert a bias bar into the sewn tube. Slide the bar through the tube as you press the stem flat to one side (not open), centering the seam allowances so they won't be visible from the front **(fig. 25).** Because of the seam-allowance differences that can occur, the best bias-bar width for each project can vary from person to person, even for stems of the same size. Ultimately, I've found it's best to simply choose a bar that will fit comfortably into the sewn tube.

Fig. 23 Fold a bias strip in half, *wrong* sides together, and stitch a scant ¼" from the long edges.

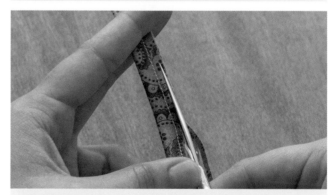

Fig. 24 Trim the seam allowances of strips cut 1"-wide or less.

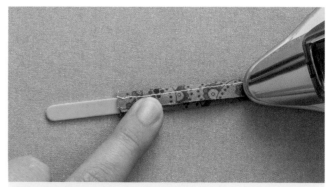

Fig. 25 Slide a bias bar through the fabric tube as you press the seam allowances to one side.

• PIN POINT •

Joining Strips with Straight Seams

Experience has taught me that joining pieced strips for bias-tube stems or vines with straight seams (rather than diagonal seams) will enable you to easily press the bias tubes flat with a bias bar. Simply slide the bias bar through your sewn tube in the direction the seams have been pressed, and it will pass through easily without becoming caught on the seams.

4. Remove the bias bar and place small dots of liquid basting glue at approximately ½" intervals underneath the layers of the pressed seam allowances **(fig. 26)**. Use a hot, dry iron on the wrong side of the stem, allowing it to rest on each area of the stem for two or three seconds, to heat set the glue and anchor the seam allowances in place.

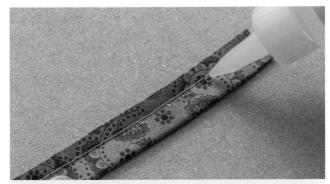

Fig. 26 Dot the stem under the seam allowance with liquid basting glue.

• PIN POINT •

Hidden Seam Allowances

If it appears that your seam allowances are too wide to be hidden from the front of the stem as you are pressing it flat with the bias bar, try pressing it again after the bar has been removed. The benefit of the bar is that it enables the stem to easily be pressed flat, but removing it eliminates the bulk it can add when inserted, and you'll now see the accurate resting position of your seam allowances.

• PIN POINT •

Creating Dimension with Seam Allowances

Unless there's a chance the seam allowances will be visible from the front of my stems, I don't trim them, as the added layers of fabric will slightly puff up the finished stems for a beautiful dimensional look. In addition, leaving the seam allowances intact enables the stems to be glue basted along the top of the seam-allowance layers for design layout, without the possibility that the glue dots will soak through to the top of the stem, and the finished stems will have smooth, flawless curves.

"Homestead Harvest," from Simple Appeal

"Geese in the Garden," from Simple Blessings

Basting Appliqués

Invisible machine appliqué, like traditional needle-turn appliqué, is sewn in layers from the bottom to the top. Keep in mind as you position and baste your appliqués that it's generally a good practice to leave approximately ½" between the outermost appliqués of your design and the raw edges of your background fabric, because this will preserve an intact margin of space around each piece after the quilt top has been assembled.

Glue basting is my preferred method for anchoring the appliqués, because it's quicker than thread basting or pinning, there are no pins to stitch around, and the appliqués won't shift or cause the background to shrink as they're stitched.

1. Lay out the prepared appliqués on the background to ensure that everything fits and is to your liking. As you position the pieces, remember that any appliqué with a raw edge that will be overlapped by another piece (such as a stem) should be overlapped by approximately ¼" to prevent fraying.

2. Remove all but the bottom appliqués and baste them in place. Without shifting the appliqué from its position, fold over one half of the shape to expose the back and place small dots of liquid basting glue along the fabric seam allowance (not the freezer-paper pattern piece) at approximately ½" intervals **(fig. 27).** If the shape has a point, always be sure to position a dot of glue in the center of the seam allowance at the point, as this will help the appliqué remain securely in place during the stitching process.

3. Firmly push the basted portion of the appliqué onto the background with your hand **(fig. 28).** Fold back the unbasted half of the appliqué and glue baste the remaining portion of the seam allowance. From the back of your work, use a hot, dry iron (I use the cotton setting) to heat set and dry the dots of glue and firmly anchor the appliqué in place.

Fig. 27 Dot the seam allowance with liquid fabric glue.

Fig. 28 Firmly push the appliqué into position on the background fabric with your hand.

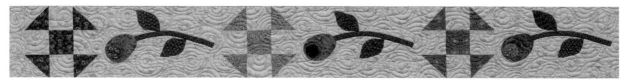

"Fresh Cut Flowers," from Simple Charm

Choosing Monofilament Thread

Monofilament thread (sometimes called *invisible thread),* which I use for invisible machine appliqué, is available in nylon and polyester. Both types have their own characteristics and strengths and bring different benefits to your appliqué projects.

In my experience, nylon thread tends to produce results that are slightly more invisible, but extra care should be used as your project is being assembled and pressed because this thread can be weakened by the heat of a very hot iron. For best results when working with nylon thread, avoid applying prolonged or high heat directly to the front of your appliqués and press any nearby seams with care. Once the project is finished and bound, I've found that the stitched appliqués will stand up well to everyday use and care. When I use nylon monofilament for my own projects, I've had very good results using the YLI brand.

If you'd like an extra measure of confidence that your appliqués will remain securely in place, even if they're inadvertently pressed from the front and exposed to direct heat from your iron, you may wish to use polyester monofilament thread. I find that the look of polyester monofilament can vary greatly from one brand to another, with some brands appearing less transparent, heavier, or even shinier than others. Depending upon the brand you choose, the monofilament may be slightly more visible on your stitched appliqués. For projects where I've opted to use a polyester product, I've been very pleased with the Sulky brand, because I feel the results most closely resemble those that are achieved when using nylon monofilament.

Ultimately, I don't feel there is one "best" type of thread. I recommend that you experiment with both types of monofilament and make this decision based upon your own personal results and preferences.

"Starberry Jam," from Simple Appeal

"Prairie Star Posies," from Homestyle Quilts, *coauthored with Laurie Baker*

Preparing Your Sewing Machine

Monofilament thread produces results that are nearly invisible, and it's easy to use once you know the best settings for your sewing machine. Always match your monofilament thread to your appliqué, not your background—you'll find that the smoke color will generally be the best choice for medium and dark prints, and the clear color works well for bright colors and pastels. If you're not sure which color is the best choice, lay a strand of each thread over your appliqué fabric to audition them.

1. Use a size 75/11 (or smaller) machine quilting needle in your sewing machine and thread it with monofilament. If possible, use an upright spool-pin position on your sewing machine for the monofilament, as this will facilitate a smooth, even feed.

2. Wind the bobbin with neutral-colored thread. In my experience, a 50-weight (or heavier) thread works well for this technique in most sewing machines, as it will resist sliding through the fabric and pulling up to the surface of your appliqués. Also, keep in mind that pre-wound bobbins, while convenient, can sometimes make it difficult to achieve perfectly balanced tension for this technique.

Note: If your machine's bobbin case features a special eye for use with embroidery techniques, threading the bobbin thread through this opening will often provide additional tension control to perfectly regulate your stitches.

3. Set your sewing machine to the zigzag stitch, adjust the width and length to achieve a tiny stitch as shown below (keeping in mind that your inner stitches should land two or three threads inside your appliqué, with your outer stitches piercing the background immediately next to the appliqué). Also reduce the tension setting. For many sewing machines, a stitch width and length setting of 1 and a tension setting of 1 to 2 produces the perfect stitch.

Approximate stitch size

• PIN POINT •

Eliminating Visible Needle Holes

I've discovered that solid fabrics, prints with a very subtle texture, and batiks (because of the tight weave this type of cloth features) can often show needle holes that are more visible than desired after the appliqués have been stitched. If this result occurs, try substituting a smaller needle for your future pieces (such as a Universal size 60/8) for less visible stitches.

• PIN POINT •

Stitch Sizes Aren't Universal

In the course of working with a huge variety of sewing machines while teaching invisible-machine-appliqué workshops, I've learned one very important lesson: stitch sizes aren't universal! The stitching guidelines I've shared in this section are a great starting point as you experiment with your machine, but keep in mind that any given stitch produced by a particular sewing machine may be different than the same programmed stitch produced by another machine. Your ultimate goal is to set the stitch size so that the appliqué edges are secured well, with the inner stitch landing a couple threads inside the perimeter of the shape and the outer stitch dropping into the background cloth exactly next to the appliqué edge.

Stitching the Appliqués

Before stitching your first invisible-machine-appliqué project, I recommend experimenting with a simple pattern shape (such as a leaf) to become comfortable with this technique and find the best settings for your sewing machine. Keep your test piece as a quick reference for future projects, making a note directly on the background fabric as to your machine's width, length, and tension settings. If you use a variety of all-purpose threads in your quiltmaking, you may also wish to note the type of thread used in your bobbin, because using a different thread can affect the balance you've achieved and your settings may need to be tweaked.

1. Slide the basted appliqué under the sewing-machine needle from the front to the back to direct the threads behind the machine, positioning a straight or gently curved edge under the needle. I always position my appliqués so they rest to the left of the needle, just as I do for my patchwork **(fig. 29)**.

2. Place your fingertip over the monofilament tail or grasp the threads to anchor them as your machine takes two or three stitches. Release the threads and continue zigzag stitching around your shape, with the inner stitches landing two or three threads inside the appliqué and the outer stitches piercing the background immediately next to the appliqué **(fig. 30)**.

To maintain good control as you work your way around each shape, stitch at a slow to moderate speed, stopping and pivoting as often as needed to keep the edge of the appliqué feeding straight toward the needle. As you work your way around the shape, train your eyes to watch the outer stitches to keep your appliqué positioned correctly, and the inner stitches will naturally fall into place.

Fig. 29 Position the appliqué to the left of the needle with the thread tails smoothed toward the back of the machine.

Fig. 30 Set your zigzag stitch so the inner stitches land two or three threads inside the appliqué and the outer stitches pierce the background right next to the appliqué.

• PIN POINT •

Pivot Inside the Appliqué

Experience has taught me that pivoting the shape with the needle down inside the appliqué, rather than in the background, is best, as the freezer-paper pattern piece will help stabilize the appliqué to prevent the shape from becoming distorted and the needle holes aren't as likely to stretch and become too visible as you stitch your design.

3. After a short distance, pause and carefully clip the monofilament tail close to the background to prevent it from becoming caught in your line of stitching **(fig. 31).**

4. Check your stitches to make sure the tension is correct. If dots of bobbin thread appear along the top surface edge of your appliqué as you stitch, this is generally because the thread tension is too tight **(fig. 32).** If this occurs, further adjust the tension settings on your machine (usually lower) until the bobbin threads disappear.

Your stitch should look like a true zigzag pattern on both the front and back of your work. If the monofilament thread is raised on the back, with an obvious "plastic" feel, or the stitches appear loose or loopy, adjust the tension settings (usually higher) until the stitches are secure **(fig. 33).**

5. To firmly secure an inner appliqué point, stitch to the position where the inner stitch rests just inside the inner point of the appliqué and stop. Pivot the fabric, and with the appliqué inner point at a right angle to the needle, continue stitching. For pieces with inner points that seem delicate, I often give a little resistance to my piece as it's feeding under the needle; this enables the machine to drop an extra stitch or two into this area and secure it well.

Fig. 31 Clip the thread tail close to the background.

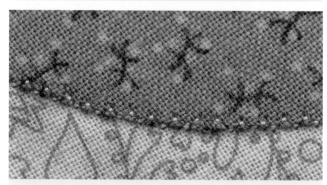

Fig. 32 Reduce the thread tension if you see dots of bobbin thread on the top of your appliqué.

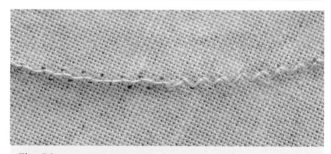

Fig. 33 Increase your thread tension if the stitches appear loose on the back of the work.

Stop and pivot.

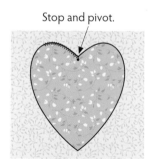

Continue stitching.

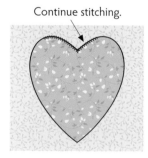

• PIN POINT •

Adjusting the Tension

Because each sewing machine is different, the best setting for the thread tension can vary greatly from one machine to another, even for machines of the same make and model. As you experiment to find your own ideal settings, it's best to simply raise or lower the tension level until the machine is achieving the desired results. Don't be overly concerned about the setting numbers—they're just numbers!

6. To secure an outer point, stitch to the position where the outer stitch lands in the background exactly next to the appliqué point and stop. With the needle in the down position in the background, pivot the fabric and continue stitching along the next side of the shape. As you begin sewing again, a second stitch will drop into the point of the appliqué.

Stop and pivot.

Continue stitching.

7. Continue stitching around the edge of the appliqué until you overlap your starting position by approximately ¼". End with a locking stitch if your machine offers this feature, placing the stitch on either the appliqué or the background, wherever it will best be hidden. For machines without a locking stitch, extend your overlapped area to be about ½" and your appliqué will remain well secured. I've discovered that using a locking stitch to finish each appliqué communicates to your sewing machine that you've finished your current task and enables you to easily position your next appliqué for stitching, because the needle will consistently align and begin in the same position. If your sewing machine doesn't feature a locking stitch, simply take your first stitch to determine where the needle will land, reposition your appliqué if needed to align it correctly, and continue zigzag stitching.

• PIN POINT •

Evaluating Stitch Placement

As you become familiar with this invisible-machine-appliqué technique, it's a good idea to evaluate your stitch placement to ensure you're achieving the most secure and invisible results possible. To do this, hold a completed appliqué piece under a ceiling light or in front of a window and view it with the light shining from behind. A properly stitched appliqué will have a ring of tiny needle holes encircling the appliqué in the background cloth. If your results are different, then adjust the placement of your work under the needle as you stitch future pieces.

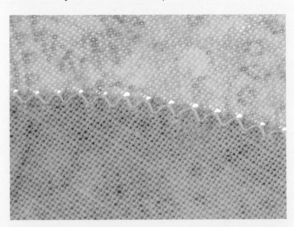

Needle holes should be visible around the perimeter of the appliqué when the piece is held up to the light.

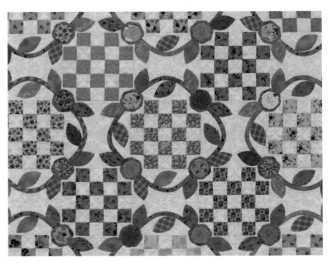

"Country Wedding Ring," from Simple Seasons

String Appliqué

When two or more appliqués are in close proximity on the same layer, I recommend stitching your first appliqué as previously instructed, but instead of clipping the threads when you finish stitching, lift the presser foot and slide the background to the next appliqué without lifting it from the sewing-machine surface. Lower the presser foot and resume stitching the next appliqué, remembering to end with a locking stitch or overlap your starting position by ¼" to ½". After the cluster of appliqués has been stitched, carefully clip the threads between each.

Removing Paper Pattern Pieces

Please note that the steps provided here are only needed for appliqués that contain freezer-paper pattern pieces; it isn't necessary to cut away the back of any shape (such as a stem) that doesn't contain paper.

1. On the wrong side of the stitched appliqué, use embroidery scissors with a sharp point to carefully pinch and cut through the fabric at least ¼" inside the appliqué seam **(fig. 34).** Trim away the background fabric, leaving a generous ¼" seam allowance **(fig. 35).**

Fig. 34 Use tip of scissors to snip into the background fabric only.

Fig. 35 Trim away the background fabric under the appliqué, leaving a generous ¼" seam allowance.

• PIN POINT •

Removing the Paper behind Small Circles

Because of their size, small circles can sometimes present a challenge when it comes to removing paper pattern pieces. For designs that include these elements, I've found that it's always best to cut away a small circle in the center of the background under the shape (think Lifesaver!) rather than cutting a slit, because there's always a small chance that slits can run and become enlarged as you work with the shape. For these small shapes, I've found that a cuticle pusher is perfect for loosening the pattern piece, and with the small size of this tool, there's less chance that your background fabric will tear.

"Serendipity Sampler," from Simple Comforts

2. Grasp the appliqué edge between the thumb and finger of one hand and grab the seam allowances immediately opposite with the thumb and fingers of your other hand **(fig. 36).** Give a gentle but firm tug to free the paper edge.

3. Use your fingertip to loosen the small amount of glue anchoring the center of the pattern piece to the fabric; if it's difficult to slide your finger between the layers, you're likely using a bit too much glue stick to anchor the freezer-paper pattern pieces to the cloth, and you'll want to adjust this for future appliqués.

4. Work your way around the shape to remove the pattern piece, pulling the paper straight out from the stitched edge, and discard it **(fig. 37).** Any paper that remains in the appliqué corners can be pulled out with a pair of tweezers—if the paper piece is too small to see or easily grasp, it isn't worth worrying about!

Fig. 36 Grasp the appliqué and seam allowance edges with the thumb and fingers of both hands and give a gentle tug to free the paper.

Fig. 37 Loosen the glued area of the pattern piece from the fabric and pull the paper away from the line of stitching.

"Colonial Cockscomb," from Simple Blessings

Completing the Machine-Appliqué Process

Always work from the bottom layer to the top as you build and stitch your designs, remembering to remove the paper pattern pieces after each new layer has been stitched. Keep in mind that it isn't necessary to stitch any appliqué edge that will be overlapped by another piece. If needed, *briefly* press your finished work from the back to ensure the seam allowances will lie smooth and flat after the paper pattern pieces have been removed. Always take care not to apply direct heat to the front of your appliqués, as this could weaken the monofilament threads.

• PIN POINT •

Safe, Secure, and Soft

Please rest easy knowing that cutting away the center of the fabric behind your appliqués won't weaken the quilt top in any way—this method of invisible machine appliqué is very secure, especially with the generous ¼" seam allowance that's left in place after cutting away the center. Using this method will result in finished projects that remain soft and pliable, even for designs with multiple layers.

Troubleshooting

Once you're familiar with this invisible-machine-appliqué technique, things should go like clockwork—your projects can be completed in much less time than traditional needle-turn methods, and your finished appliqués will feature stitches that are invisible, sturdy, and secure.

Because we all occasionally experience little bumps in the road (yes, I do too!), here are a handful of tips and tricks I've learned through the years to help things continue to run smoothly.

PROBLEM	QUICK FIX
Monofilament isn't feeding smoothly	After you've found your perfect sewing-machine settings, if your monofilament thread isn't feeding well and you begin to hear a clunky "not happy" noise from your machine, check your spool of thread. Monofilament is a bit stretchy, so it can occasionally become wrapped around the spool pin. Simply unwind and properly reposition the monofilament, rethread the machine, and then continue stitching.
Stitches look off-kilter	If your stitches begin looking less than perfect and your thread appears to be feeding properly from the spool pin, remove the spool of thread and the bobbin and rethread the machine. Because monofilament thread is very fine, it sometimes can become dislodged from an internal mechanism or the thread take-up lever. Rethreading the machine will generally correct this issue and your stitches will be back on track.
Tension adjustment doesn't solve bobbin thread pulling to surface	No matter how you adjust the tension level on your sewing machine, if you continue to see bobbin thread on the top surface of your appliqué, if's often because the bobbin thread is too fine or has a silky finish. While it seems logical that a fine, silky bobbin thread will result in a perfect balance when used in combination with delicate monofilament, I find that often the opposite is true. Fine sewing threads are created to easily slide through your fabrics when stitching patchwork, but this isn't the function you're looking for when stitching invisible machine appliqué. Try substituting a heavier-weight thread (Gütermann's 50-weight cotton thread works well for me, and in my experience, for most sewing machines), and your results will almost certainly improve.
Bobbin thread appears on inner edge of appliqué	When any of the above issues occasionally occur, the result can often be dots of bobbin thread that are visible along the inner edge of your appliqué. If this happens, use a fine-tipped Micron Pigma marker to place a small dot of color on the visible thread. I keep these markers in both the brown and black hues in my sewing room; these colors will disguise visible bobbin dots on nearly any print.

Alternate Thread Options

As an added design element when stitching appliqués using this invisible-machine-appliqué technique, from time to time you may wish to consider replacing the monofilament thread in your needle with standard all-purpose thread for stitches that are subtle but visible. When selecting your thread color, there are three great options to consider.

- If you have a large stash of thread, change the thread color in your needle to suit the print of each individual appliqué being stitched.

- For a little splash of color that's subtle yet effective, especially if you don't have a large selection of thread, try using variegated thread. A handful of spools that include the main hues in your quilt will complement a wide range of colors and be appropriate for a variety of prints, or you can use one multicolored spool to stitch the entire design.

- If you'd like to take a simple approach, one complementary neutral thread color can be used across the entire quilt top for the appliqué design, which will unify the color scheme nicely.

When substituting all-purpose thread for monofilament thread in your machine-appliqué projects, you'll find that it isn't necessary to adjust the tension settings for your sewing machine.

• PIN POINT •

Adhesive Labels

This may seem like a very minor thing, but I've learned to completely remove the adhesive labels on my spools of thread rather than push the spool pin through the label and into the opening. If you leave the label in place, the adhesive can rub off onto the spool pin and negatively affect the feed of the thread. Taking a moment to remove the label will help ensure the thread feeds smoothly through your sewing machine.

"Cottage Garden Table Runner and Penny Mug Mats," from Simple Graces

Invisible Machine Appliqué with Trapunto

Trapunto *is a style of embellishing* appliqués by slightly stuffing them for a dimensional appearance. Adding trapunto accents to appliqué designs that have already been stitched using the invisible-machine-appliqué technique is incredibly easy to do, and your finished projects will definitely be attention-getters.

Materials

In addition to the supplies noted (page 8) for invisible machine appliqué, you'll need the following tools and supplies for this technique:

- Low-loft quilt batting
- Fine-tip water-soluble marker

Adding Trapunto Accents

After completing any given appliqué project using the technique outlined in "Invisible Machine Appliqué" (page 8), it's easy to add stuffed accents. Keep in mind that you'll only want to add these accents to shapes with a single layer, or to the topmost shapes in layered appliqué designs.

1. After selecting the appliqué you wish to stuff, use the shape's corresponding appliqué template and a fine-tip water-soluble marker to trace the pattern onto a piece of low-loft quilt batting **(fig. 1)**.

2. Using embroidery scissors with a fine, sharp point, cut out the batting shape along the *inside* of the drawn line **(fig. 2)**. Cutting inside the drawn line will result in a batting piece that's slightly smaller than the appliqué, to ensure it fits well.

"Petal Pusher," from Simple Graces

Fig. 1 Use the template to trace the shape onto the batting.

Fig. 2 Cut out the shape *inside* the drawn line.

3. From the wrong side of the completed appliqué block or unit, insert the batting shape under the stitched appliqué. Use an awl or stiletto to tuck the batting edges under the seam allowance that remains after removing the paper pattern piece **(fig. 3)**.

Fig. 3 Insert the batting shape under the stitched appliqué.

> **• PIN POINT •**
>
> ### Batting Loft
>
> Thin batting will provide a stuffed but subtle look to your appliqués while enabling the block to lie smooth and flat. For a more dramatic effect, you can use a slightly thicker batting, but I suggest doing a quick test using a sample appliqué piece to ensure the background will still remain smooth and flat after the appliqués have been stuffed.

4. Apply small dots of liquid basting glue around the edge of the batting at approximately ½" intervals, ensuring the glue dots are positioned under the appliqué seam allowance **(fig. 4)**.

Fig. 4 Apply glue dots to the batting under the appliqué seam allowance.

5. From the back of the block or unit, use the point of a hot, dry iron (I use the cotton setting) to heat set the glue dots and anchor the batting piece firmly in place **(fig. 5)**. Take care to use the point of the iron only, and avoid applying heat to the line of stitches along the appliqué edge so they don't become weakened.

Completing the Trapunto Process

Once the appliqués have been stuffed with the batting shapes, the final step is to layer your quilt top with the batting and backing and quilt the layers. The quilting process will ensure the batting shapes in the stuffed appliqués remain firmly in place without shifting, and after quilting, your appliqué design will have a beautiful, dimensional appearance.

Fig. 5 Use the point of the iron to heat set the glue.

> **• PIN POINT •**
>
> ### Seam-Allowance Security
>
> While I typically use this trapunto method for projects that have been stitched using my invisible-machine-appliqué technique, it will also work for other appliqué methods. As long as there's a strip of seam allowance on the back of the finished appliqué shape to help hold the batting piece in place, you're good to go!

Needle-Turn Appliqué

Needle turn is a traditional hand-stitched appliqué method that has long been favored by quiltmakers. For this technique, shapes are traced and cut from fabric and the seam allowances are turned under as the appliqués are stitched in place. If you enjoy the comfort of handwork and love projects that are portable, this is an ideal method for stitching your appliqué designs.

Materials

In addition to standard quiltmaking supplies, the following tools and products are needed for this method:

- Embroidery scissors with a fine, sharp point
- Fine-weight thread in colors to match your appliqués
- Freezer paper
- Marking tools, such as a quilter's silver pencil or fine-tip water-soluble marker
- Size 9 or 10 straw needles (or a size that fits comfortably in your hand)

  Note: Straw needles feature a longer length that's easy to grasp, and they enable you to turn under and stitch your appliqués neatly while maintaining a good level of control as you work with the appliqué fabric.

- Thimble (leather thimbles work well for this technique because they offer a degree of flexibility).

Preparing the Appliqués for Stitching

1. To easily trace the appliqué shapes for cutting and stitching, prepare a tracing template of each pattern in your project as instructed in "Preparing Pattern Tracing Templates" (page 9).

"Four Patch Potpourri," from Homestyle Quilts, *coauthored with Laurie Baker*

"Summertime Scatter Garden" from Simple Seasons

2. Using a quilter's silver pencil or a fine-tip water-soluble marker (white markers show up well on medium and dark prints; blue markers are easily visible on lighter prints), lay the templates on the right side of the fabrics and trace the shapes exactly around the paper edges the number of times indicated by the pattern **(fig. 1)**. If you're tracing more than one shape onto the same fabric, leave at least ½" between the shapes. Typically, I position my shapes with the longest lines or curves on the diagonal grain of the cloth, because the resulting bias edges are easier to work with. However, if I wish to take advantage of directional prints or stripes, then I disregard this guideline and position the shapes in a way that pleases me.

3. Using embroidery scissors with a fine, sharp point, cut out the traced shapes, adding a scant ¼" seam allowance on all sides **(fig. 2)**.

Incorporating Bias-Tube Stems and Vines

As a matter of personal preference, I use bias-tube stems and vines for all of my appliqué designs, no matter what appliqué method I'm using, because they eliminate the need to turn under seam-allowance edges as the lengths are stitched to the background. To prepare bias tubes, refer to "Making Bias-Tube Stems and Vines" (page 18).

Laying Out and Stitching Needle-Turn Appliqué Designs

1. Lay out the appliqué design to ensure everything fits and is to your liking, leaving approximately ½" between the outermost appliqués and the edge of the background fabric. When you're pleased with the arrangement, remove all but the bottommost pieces. Pin or thread baste the appliqués in place, placing the pins or basting stitches well away from the outer edges where the shapes will be stitched **(fig. 3)**.

Fig. 1 Trace the template shape onto the right side of the fabric.

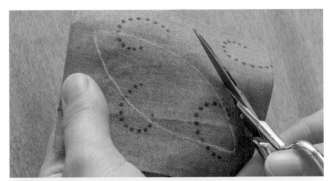
Fig. 2 Add a scant ¼" seam allowance as you cut out the traced shape.

Fig. 3 Pin or thread baste the appliqués to the background fabric.

• PIN POINT •

Basting with White Thread

When thread basting my appliqués, I've found it's best to use a needle and a single strand of white thread, because colored threads can sometimes leave a residue of tinted fibers in the cloth of your appliqués. Best of all, the white thread is easily visible on most prints, making it easy to remove the basting stitches after your design is complete.

2. Thread a straw needle with fine-weight thread (approximately 18" in length) in a color to match your appliqué; if you aren't able to perfectly match the color of your print, it's generally best to choose a shade that's very slightly darker, as it will blend nicely and be less visible after stitching. Tie a double knot near the end of the thread by forming a small loop, rolling the end of the thread through the loop twice, and pulling up the slack.

3. If you're right-handed, work from right to left as you stitch your appliqués; if you're left-handed, reverse the direction and work from left to right. Beginning at a straight or gently curved edge, use the tip of your needle to gently grab the seam allowance and sweep it under the appliqué, stopping at the inside edge of the traced line **(fig. 4).**

4. Use your thumb and finger to gently but firmly hold the turned-under portion of seam allowance in place. With your other hand, bring the needle up from the wrong side of the background through the appliqué, catching a couple of threads on the edge **(fig. 5).** Pull the threaded needle until the knot is flush with the background; the knot will be hidden under the appliqué.

5. For sturdy yet invisible stitches, insert the needle into the background cloth about a thread behind the point where the sewing thread feeds up from the background cloth. Bring the point of the needle back up and through the turned edge of the appliqué, just in front of the previous stitch, catching a couple of threads **(fig. 6).** Pull up the slack until the thread nestles into the appliqué.

Fig. 4 Use the tip of the needle to sweep under the seam allowance.

Fig. 5 Bring the needle from the back to the surface, catching a couple of threads on the edge of the appliqué.

Fig. 6 Insert the needle into the background next to where it came out, and then into the edge of the appliqué.

• PIN POINT •

Protecting Your Fingers

To protect your fingertip as you push the needle through the cloth and take your stitches, I suggest using a thimble. I've found leather thimbles to be a great choice, as they aren't as bulky as metal thimbles and they enable you to easily push the needle through the cloth without slipping.

• PIN POINT •

Stitching Dimensional Stems and Vines

For finished stems and vines with a beautiful raised appearance that resemble trapunto (appliqués that have been stuffed for a dimensional look; see page 30), I stitch my bias-tube stems and vines using the same stitch described in steps 5 and 6 on page 34 and below (minus the step of turning under the seam allowances), but with one small adjustment.

Instead of inserting my threaded needle exactly next to the stem into the background cloth as I take my stitches, I reach a thread or two *under* the stem when inserting the needle. Placing your stitches slightly under the edge of the stems has the effect of drawing the outer portion of the stems slightly downward, while also puffing up the centers. This little trick is easy and simple to do, and the results are stunning.

6. Continue turning under the appliqué edge and stitching the shape to the background as previously instructed, turning under and stitching about ¼" of the appliqué seam allowance at a time.

7. For perfectly formed inner points and curves, clip the seam allowance once at the center of the curve or point, stopping a couple of threads away from the inner edge of the drawn line **(fig. 7).**

Fig. 7 Clip the seam allowance at the center position of inner points and curves.

"Passing Fancy," from Simple Traditions

8. Use the tip of the needle to sweep under the seam allowance approaching the clip, holding it in place with your thumb and finger; stitch the turned-under edge nearly to the position of the clip, stopping about a stitch away **(fig. 8)**.

9. Turn under the remaining side of the seam allowance at the point of the clip using the tip of your needle. Take a stitch or two to secure this delicate area and continue stitching around the shape **(fig. 9)**.

10. For sharp outer points, turn under and stitch the seam allowance leading up to the point, placing your last stitch at the point **(fig. 10)**.

11. Use the tip of your needle to sweep under the seam allowance on the remaining side of the point, and continue stitching until the entire appliqué has been secured to the background **(fig. 11)**.

Fig. 8 Stop stitching about one stitch away from clip.

Fig. 9 Take one or two stitches at the point of the clip.

Fig. 10 Turn under the seam allowance up to the point, placing the last stitch at the point.

Fig. 11 Turn under the seam allowance on the remaining side of the point and continue stitching.

"Quaint and Charming," from Simple Traditions

• PIN POINT •

Stitching Sharp Points

For beautifully shaped points, try this little trick. After turning under the seam allowance on the remaining side of the appliqué, take an extra stitch exactly at the point, inserting the needle into the background fabric just a thread or two outside the point, before continuing around the shape. This extra stitch will help elongate and sharpen your points so they always look crisp and precise.

Take an extra stitch at the tip of outer points.

12. To end your stitching, insert the needle into the background fabric exactly next to the finished appliqué, bringing it to the wrong side of your work. Take a small stitch under the appliqué just a bit in from the edge, taking care not to come up through the surface of the appliqué, and pull the thread until a small loop remains **(fig. 12)**. Pass your needle through the loop and pull up the slack to form a knot. To ensure the knotted thread will remain secure, I repeat this process to make a second knot, and then clip the thread.

13. Continue working from the bottom layer to the top to position, baste, and stitch the remaining pieces in your appliqué design, ensuring that the edges of any overlapped pieces do so by about ¼" to prevent fraying.

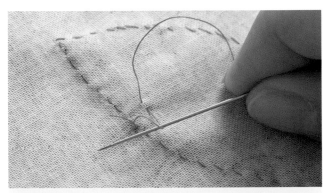

Fig. 12 Take a small stitch about ¼" in from the edge of the appliqué and pull the thread until a small loop remains.

"Passing Fancy," from Simple Traditions

Fusion Appliqué

Fusion appliqué *is my term* for designs that are stitched using a combination of elements—both invisible machine appliqué and traditional needle-turn appliqué. What I love about this method is that you can prepare the appliqués in advance with the edges turned under, and then the design can be basted in place for quick hand stitching. Because the appliqué edges have already been turned under, this technique enables you to make swift progress for a perfect blend of modern convenience and tradition.

Materials

In addition to your standard quiltmaking supplies, the following tools and products are needed for this method:

- Awl or stiletto with a *sharp* point
- Bias bars in various widths (for designs featuring stems and vines)
- Embroidery scissors with a fine, sharp point
- Fine-weight thread in colors to match your appliqués
- Freezer paper
- Glue stick for fabric, water-soluble and acid-free
- Iron with a sharp pressing point (travel-sized or mini appliqué irons work well for this technique)
- Liquid fabric glue, water-soluble and acid-free (my favorite brand is Quilter's Choice by Beacon Adhesives)
- Marking tools, such as a quilter's silver pencil or fine-tip water-soluble markers
- Pressing board with a *firm* surface
- Size 9 or 10 straw needles (or a size that fits comfortably in your hand)

  Note: Straw needles feature a longer length that's easy to grasp and will help you maintain a good level of control as you work with the cloth.
- Thimble (leather thimbles work well for this technique)
- Tweezers with rounded tips

"Feathered Stars," from Simple Traditions

Preparing and Stitching the Appliqués

1. Referring to "Invisible Machine Appliqué" (page 8), follow the steps to prepare the templates, freezer-paper pattern pieces, and appliqués specified in your project.

2. Lay out your appliqué design on the background to ensure everything fits and is to your liking. When you're pleased with the arrangement, remove all but the bottommost pieces.

3. Referring to "Basting Appliqués" (page 20), use liquid fabric glue to baste the seam allowance of the appliqués and position them on the background. Remember to heat set the glue-basted design from the back of your work, because this will ensure the appliqués stay firmly in place as you stitch them.

4. If you're right-handed, you'll want to work from right to left as you stitch your appliqués; if you're left-handed, reverse the direction and work from left to right. Beginning at a straight or gently curved edge and using a straw needle with a knotted length (approximately 18") of fine-weight thread in a color to match your appliqué, bring the needle up from the back of your work, catching a couple of threads along the edge of the appliqué **(fig. 1)**. Pull the threaded needle until the knot is flush with the background; this will hide the knot under the appliqué.

5. Insert the needle into the background about a thread behind the point where the sewing thread feeds up from the background cloth. Bring the point of the needle back up through the edge of the appliqué, just in front of the previous stitch, catching a couple of threads along the prepared edge of the shape **(fig. 2)**. Pull up the slack until the thread nestles into the appliqué fabric.

Fig. 1 Bring the needle up from the back to the front of the work, catching a couple of threads along the edge of the appliqué.

Fig. 2 Insert the needle into the background next to where the thread feeds up through the fabric and then into the edge of the appliqué.

"Gathering Garden," from Simple Charm

39

6. To achieve a finished appliqué that will remain securely in place when the paper pattern piece is removed, take tiny, closely spaced stitches as you work your way around the shape.

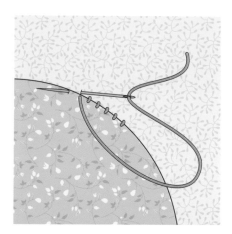

Fig. 3 Cut away the excess fabric beneath each appliqué and remove the paper pattern piece.

7. Complete the stitching for all appliqués included in the current design layer, ending the stitching for each as described in step 12 of "Laying Out and Stitching Needle-Turn Appliqué Designs" (page 33). Referring to "Removing Paper Pattern Pieces" (page 26), cut away the excess fabric beneath each appliqué and carefully remove the paper pattern pieces **(fig. 3)**.

8. Continue working from the bottom layer to the top as you position, baste, and stitch your designs, remembering to remove the paper pattern pieces before adding each new layer. If needed, *briefly* press your finished work from the back to ensure the seam allowances lie smooth and flat.

• PIN POINT •

Perforating the Pattern Piece

Although it may seem like you're not securing much of the appliqué as you stitch through the side edges of your shape, remember that because the seam allowance has been turned under, you're catching twice the number of threads as your needle passes through the folded edge of cloth. Taking closely spaced stitches along the perimeter of appliqué means that your needle will nick the paper pattern piece edge, perforating it for easy removal when your stitching is complete.

"Bloomin' Wonderful," from Simple Comforts

Wool Appliqué

Felted wool is a really fun, fast, and forgiving cloth to work with. Because wool doesn't ravel, it isn't necessary to turn under the edges of felted-wool appliqués, making it an incredibly approachable technique with a very short learning curve. My very favorite wool projects are those that combine wool appliqués with cotton fabrics, so the steps provided in this section feature this approach. Of course, wool appliqués can easily be stitched onto wool backgrounds—simply swap out your cotton background pieces and substitute wool in comparable sizes. If you haven't previously worked with wool, prepare to become addicted!

Materials

In addition to your standard quiltmaking supplies, you'll need the following tools and products for this method:

- #8 or #12 perle cotton in colors to match or complement your wool (Valdani's variegated #12 perle cotton is my favorite)
- Embroidery needle (a size 5 works well for me)
- Freezer paper
- Liquid fabric glue, water-soluble and acid-free (my favorite brand is Quilter's Choice by Beacon Adhesives)
- Paper-backed fusible web (I like the results achieved with HeatnBond Lite)
- Embroidery scissors with a fine, sharp point
- Thimble (leather thimbles work well for this technique)

"Penny Garland," from Simple Appeal

Felted-Wool Basics

Felted wool is typically used when incorporating wool appliqué into quilts and other projects. Wool that's been felted has a soft, densely woven feel to the cloth, and it resists raveling as you work with it. I suggest using only 100% wool, and as a general rule, avoid worsted wool because it doesn't felt well and can be challenging to work with. You can usually identify worsted wool by its hard, flat weave, and you'll often find it used for garments such as men's suits.

Sometimes it can be difficult to tell if wool has been felted. If I'm buying wool that's been overdyed (these pieces will often include plaids, checks, and stripes that have been dyed on top of the original woven design for added color), I always assume that simply by nature of the overdye process, the wool has been felted.

Felting Your Wool

If your wool hasn't been felted, if it features a loose weave, or if you're unsure whether it's been felted, it's easy to felt it yourself.

Wash similarly hued wool pieces in the washing machine on the longest cycle using a hot-water wash and a cold-water rinse. (You may wish to skim the surface of the water once or twice during the cycle to prevent loose fibers from clogging the drain.) Next, dry the wool in your dryer, again using the longest and hottest setting. Remove the dry wool promptly, folding large pieces into smaller, more manageable sizes to help prevent wrinkles from forming.

As an added safety measure, I always wash and dry vividly colored pieces separately when I suspect they might lose dye, and I *never* wash wool that's been overdyed, because it will almost certainly bleed color. If I'm not sure whether a piece has been overdyed, I follow the rule that it's better to be safe and ask at the time of purchase rather than to guess and be sorry. Finally, never wash wool that's been included as part of a kitted project, because it can continue to shrink and you may find yourself without enough wool to complete your design.

Wool-Appliqué Basics

When working with wool, I like using a fusible-appliqué technique for the preparation steps, liquid fabric glue for basting the layers of wool together, and perle cotton and an embroidery needle to hand stitch the pieces. These choices are a result of years of trial and error while teaching myself this technique, and they produce sturdy, neat results.

Because wool can vary in thickness, I've found that paper-backed fusible web used alone often isn't enough to hold the layers together as you work with them. The combination of fusible web and liquid glue produces ideal results because the fusible web finishes and stabilizes the underside of the wool edges to reduce fraying, while the glue-basted edges hold the layers of wool together beautifully for easy stitching without pinning.

Preparing Templates for Wool Appliqué

Keep in mind when you're working with wool appliqués and using the technique that follows, that any shape that isn't perfectly symmetrical will appear backward and be reversed from the original pattern once it has been stitched.

To simplify preparation and enable any given appliqué to easily be positioned in the direction needed, I make a tracing template for each required shape. Having a template will enable you to easily flip it and adjust the direction when tracing patterns for your design, and you can quickly adapt the direction of any shape to suit your needs.

Referring to "Preparing Pattern Tracing Templates" (page 9), make a template of each appliqué shape needed.

Preparing the Paper-Backed Fusible-Web Shapes

For this wool appliqué method, you'll need one paper-backed fusible-web shape for each appliqué to be included in your project. To prevent the appliqués from feeling stiff and heavy, the fusible-web shapes will be prepared using a "windowing" technique, which simply means that the center of the web will be cut away.

1. Use the prepared templates to trace each shape the number of times needed onto the paper side of the fusible web **(fig. 1)**. (For projects with only a handful of shapes that don't require reversing, you can trace the shapes directly from the pattern sheet.) Leave approximately ½" between each traced shape and remember to reverse the direction of any shape that isn't perfectly symmetrical.

2. Cut out each shape approximately ¼" *outside* the drawn lines, and then cut away the center portion of each shape approximately ¼" *inside* the drawn lines to window it **(fig. 2)**.

Fig. 1 Trace each shape onto the paper side of the fusible web.

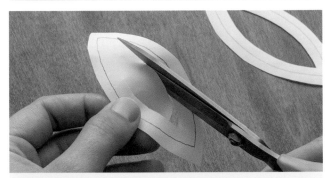

Fig. 2 Cut around the outside and inside of each shape.

• PIN POINT •

Adding Stability to Large Shapes

For added stability for large shapes, try leaving a narrow strip of paper across the middle of the shape as you cut away the excess center portion of the fusible web. This strip will act as a bridge to connect the sides and prevent any distortion as you lay out your shape onto the wool.

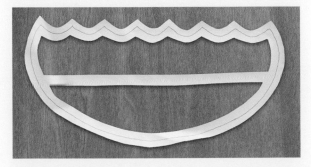

Leave a narrow strip of paper across the middle of the shape for stability.

Cutting Multiple Pieces of the Same Shape

For wool projects that include multiple appliqués made from a single pattern, I've developed a neat little shortcut that will save a tremendous amount of time when preparing the shapes from fusible web.

1. Prepare a tracing template for the needed shape as previously instructed.

2. Use the template to trace the shape onto the paper side of fusible web. Stack additional pieces of fusible web (for shapes that aren't overly complex, I suggest six pieces; for curvy shapes, try four pieces) under the top traced sheet, all with the paper side up **(fig. 3)**.

3. Anchor the layers together with a straight pin, placing it through the traced pattern line so it will be away from the area to be cut **(fig. 4)**.

4. Cut away the layered fusible-web centers ¼" *inside* the drawn line, and then cut away the background ¼" *outside* the drawn line to window the shapes **(fig. 5)**.

5. Separate the layers of fusible web. Use the template and a pencil to transfer the pattern onto the paper side of each piece under the top layer, centering it onto the windowed shape **(fig. 6)**.

This little shortcut will enable you to cut multiple pieces at a time, and having a template will make it a snap to transfer the pattern cutting lines.

"Penny-Wise" from Simple Charm

Fig. 3 Stack pieces of fusible web paper side up.

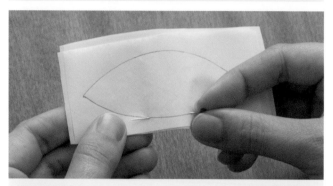

Fig. 4 Anchor layers with a straight pin placed through the traced line.

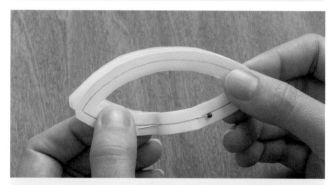

Fig. 5 Cut around the outside and inside of the drawn shape through all the layers.

Fig. 6 Use the template to transfer the pattern to each fusible-web piece.

Preparing the Wool Appliqués

1. Following the manufacturer's instructions, use a hot, dry iron (I use a low cotton setting or a high wool setting) to attach each fusible-web windowed shape, paper side up, to the wrong side of the wool **(fig. 7).** Take care not to press your shapes for too long or the fusible web may begin to disintegrate.

2. After the wool has cooled, cut out each shape exactly on the drawn lines **(fig. 8).** As you cut the wool, try angling the top blade of the scissors slightly inward toward the paper. This will bevel the appliqué edges so that the wool side is slightly larger and the fusible-web adhesive will be invisible from the front of the appliqué after stitching. Do not remove the paper backing from the wool appliqués at this time.

Fig. 7 Press each fusible-web shape onto the wrong side of the wool.

Fig. 8 Cut out each shape on the drawn lines.

• PIN POINT •

Protecting the Wool Edges from Fraying

Many times in my wool workshops, people tell me that they understand the benefit of cutting away the centers of the fusible-web shapes, but they often ask why it's helpful to leave a margin around the outside of the traced shapes as well. In a nutshell, adding a ¼" margin outside the traced lines will enable you to cut *through* the center of the stabilized portion of the wool when preparing the appliqué, instead of cutting *next* to the stabilized area, where it's more likely to fray. The resulting appliqué edges will have a crisp, sharp feel to them because they've been stabilized by the fusible-web adhesive, and any points and pronounced curves will resist raveling during the stitching process.

• PIN POINT •

Picking the Right Side

In most instances, wool doesn't have an obvious right or wrong side, but I've learned to evaluate both sides of the cloth before attaching the windowed adhesive shape. Very often wool will look different on each side, particularly if it's been overdyed, and I love being able to take advantage of the interesting variations in color that can occur. Also, when using plaids, checks, and stripes, I suggest positioning your shapes at varying angles for added texture. Doing this will make it appear as though you've incorporated a ton of different wools—a great little trick if you're just beginning to build your stash!

Sewing the Overhand Stitch

After much experimenting, I've decided that the overhand stitch is my preferred method of appliquéing wool shapes because it enables me to make quick progress, uses much less thread, and provides a softer, less-heavy look than the blanket stitch. Best of all, the stitches stay in place without rolling over the appliqué edge.

1. Use a size 5 embroidery needle threaded with a single knotted strand of #8 or #12 perle cotton (about 18" in length) to overhand stitch the appliqués as shown below. If you're right-handed, work from right to left as you stitch the shapes; if you're left-handed, simply reverse the direction and work from left to right.

Keep in mind that your stitches should be appropriate for the size of your appliqué—the smaller the shape, the shorter and more closely spaced they should be. In my opinion, it's not as important to have a uniform stitch size across the entire block or quilt top as it is to have a uniform stitch within each individual appliqué.

2. The secret to achieving evenly spaced stitches is to consistently duplicate the angle of your needle as you insert it into the appliqué and bring it up at the outside edge of the shape. The wider the angle of the needle, the farther apart your stitches will be spaced; the narrower the angle, the closer together the stitches will be **(fig. 9)**.

3. When stitching wool appliqués that feature points, I use a turkey track stitch to achieve a clean, neat look and anchor the points securely. When you estimate that you're taking your last stitch before reaching the point, insert the needle into the appliqué and bring it up just outside of the appliqué point in the background fabric. Pull the thread until it nestles into the appliqué and insert the needle back into the inner tip of the previous stitch a second time, angling it out toward the unsewn side of the point to form a mirror-image stitch. As you pull up the slack, use the needle to guide the thread loop

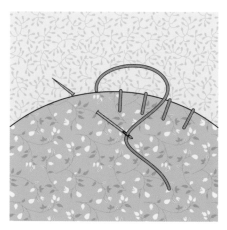

Overhand stitch

Fig. 9 The angle of the needle will determine the distance between the stitches.

"Short and Sweet," from Simple Charm

so the stitch rests exactly on the point. Insert the needle into the original stitch one last time to complete the turkey track stitch, and continue appliquéing the piece.

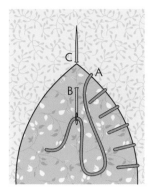

Needle up at A, down at B, and up at C

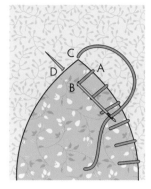

Needle down at B and up at D

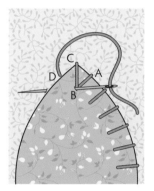

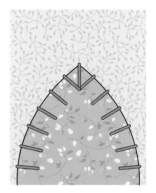

Needle down at B and continue appliquéing the piece

4. To stitch outer curves, simply angle the stitches from the outer edge toward the center of the shape so the inner portion of the stitches are spaced more closely together (think wagon wheel!) **(fig. 10).**

5. To stitch inner curves, use the technique described for outer curves, but reverse the angle of the stitches to space them more closely together along the inner curve of the appliqué and radiate them outward toward the center of the shape (wagon wheel in reverse!) **(fig. 11).**

Eliminating Background Shrinkage

Very often, the overhand stitch is sewn working from the outside of the shape toward the center. I've learned that stitching in this manner can cause the background to shrink and produce a "pillowing" effect (the appliqués take on a bit of a domed appearance), because with each stitch the needle draws the foundation fabric under and toward the center of the shape. Taking a different approach and stitching from the *inside* of the appliqué *out* will eliminate shrinkage and pillowing. With each stitch, the cloth will be drawn outward away from the center of the appliqué.

Fig. 10 Angle outer curves so the stitches are closer together inside the shape.

Fig. 11 Stitch inner curves so the stitches are closer together along the edges of the shape.

Laying Out and Stitching Wool-Appliqué Designs

For designs that include two layers or less of wool appliqués, I love the convenience of basting everything in place and having a project that's easily portable while I stitch.

When I'm working with designs that contain three or more wool layers, I work from the top layer to the bottom to stitch these layered pieces into units (such as a stack of pennies) *before* adding them to my background, because this simplifies the sewing process and eliminates the need to stitch through multiple heavy layers of wool. Once the layered units are incorporated into my design, I work from the bottom layer to the top (as is typically done with appliqué) to stitch the remaining pieces in place.

1. Lay out the appliqués, including any layered and stitched appliqué units, onto your background to ensure everything fits and is to your liking. When you're pleased with the arrangement, remove all but the bottommost pieces and remove the paper backing on each wool appliqué for the layer you're about to begin working with.

2. Referring to "Basting Appliqués" (page 20), apply small dots of liquid glue directly onto the narrow margin of adhesive that rims each shape and use a hot, dry iron to dry the glue and heat set the pieces from the back of the work **(fig. 12)**. Pressing from the back will keep the wool from taking on a shiny, flat appearance, and it will prevent any pattern or texture on the surface of the iron from transferring to the cloth.

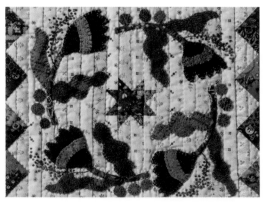

"Wreath of Lilies," from Simple Appeal

• PIN POINT •

Removing the Paper Backing

To easily remove the paper backing from the fusible web, instead of lifting up the outside edge of the paper from each wool appliqué, try using the tip of your needle to loosen the inside edge of the paper. To do this, slide the needle underneath the paper strip to hook it, and then peel it away from the shape.

Slide the needle under the edge of the paper.

Fig. 12 Heat set the glue from the back of the work.

3. Overhand stitch the appliqués that have been positioned and basted to form the first layer of the design.

4. Remove the paper backing from each wool appliqué to be included on the next layer. Lay out the appliqués, glue baste and heat set the pieces, and then stitch them in place.

5. Continue working from the bottom layer to the top to complete the design, keeping in mind that it isn't necessary to cut away the bottom layers of wool in stacked units, or the background cloth underneath wool appliqués after they've been stitched, because the thickness of the wool layers is part of the charm for this style of appliqué.

• PIN POINT •

Preventing Cotton Appliqués from Fraying

For any wool design that incorporates cotton appliqués (such as bias-tube stems and vines), ensure that the raw cotton edges are overlapped by another appliqué approximately ¼" to prevent fraying, or turn under the edges to finish them. It isn't necessary to overlap the edges of your wool appliqués unless it's an element of the design.

"Farm-Girl Finery," from Simple Appeal

Fusible Appliqué

Fusible appliqué is a fun and fast way to include appliqué designs in your quilts and projects, particularly when you don't wish to invest a huge amount of time (baby quilts are a great example). This technique is ideal for fast results, and it's especially nice for designs that include complicated shapes that would pose a challenge when turning the seam allowances under for stitching. With this technique, you'll find that any appliqué design is approachable.

Materials

In addition to standard quiltmaking supplies, you'll need the following tools and products for this method:

- Embroidery scissors with a fine, sharp point
- Freezer paper
- Open-toe presser foot
- Paper-backed fusible web (I like the results achieved when using HeatnBond Lite)
- Sewing machine capable of producing a tiny zigzag or satin stitch
- Standard sewing thread in a complementary neutral color, or individual colors to match your appliqués

Preparing Pattern Tracing Templates

For fusible-appliqué projects, any shape that isn't perfectly symmetrical will appear backward and be reversed from the original pattern once the design has been stitched.

To enable any given appliqué to be positioned in the direction needed for your project, make a tracing template for each required shape. Templates will enable you to adjust the direction of your shapes as you prepare your pattern pieces.

Referring to "Preparing Pattern Tracing Templates" (page 9), make a freezer-paper template of each required appliqué shape.

"Mocha Stars," from Simple Comforts

Preparing the Paper-Backed Fusible-Web Shapes

For this fusible-appliqué method, you'll need one traced paper-backed fusible-web shape for each appliqué to be included in your project. To prevent the appliqués from feeling stiff and heavy, prepare the fusible-web shapes using a "windowing" technique, which simply means that the center of the fusible web will be cut away.

Referring to "Preparing the Paper-Backed Fusible-Web Shapes" (page 43) and "Cutting Multiple Pieces of the Same Shape" (page 44), use the templates to prepare each shape the number of times needed.

Preparing the Fusible Appliqués

1. Following the manufacturer's instructions, use a hot, dry iron (I use the cotton setting) to attach each windowed fusible-web shape, paper side up, to the *wrong* side of the fabrics **(fig. 1).** Take care not to press the prepared shapes for too long or the fusible-web adhesive may begin to disintegrate.

2. Cut out each appliqué exactly on the drawn lines **(fig. 2).**

3. Remove the paper backing from the fusible-web that rims each piece **(fig. 3).**

Laying Out the Appliqué Design

1. Lay out the prepared appliqués, with the right side of the fabrics facing up, on the right side of the background fabric. When you're pleased with the arrangement and everything fits and is to your liking, remove all but the bottommost appliqué pieces.

2. Using a hot iron, follow the manufacturer's instructions to fuse the design to the background from the front of your work **(fig. 4).** If needed, turn the unit over and finish fusing the design from the back of the block so that the design is secure.

Fig. 1 Fuse the fusible-web shapes to the wrong side of the fabrics.

Fig. 2 Cut out each appliqué on the drawn lines.

Fig. 3 Remove the paper backing.

Fig. 4 Fuse the appliqués in place from the front of the work.

Stitching Fusible Appliqués

1. Thread the sewing-machine needle and wind the bobbin with standard all-purpose thread in a neutral color or a color to complement the appliqué to be stitched.

2. Set the sewing machine to a narrow satin stitch **(fig. 5).** To achieve this stitch on my sewing machine, I use the zigzag stitch, adjusting the width to be approximately 1⁄16" to 1⁄8" wide and setting the length for closely spaced stitches. The line of stitches should appear nearly solid.

3. Beginning with the bottommost pieces and working your way to the top, stitch each fused appliqué in place, with the outer stitches piercing the background fabric just outside the appliqué edge and the inner stitches landing approximately 1⁄16" to 1⁄8" inside the edge of the shape **(fig. 6).**

4. As you complete the stitching around each appliqué, ensure that the starting and stopping points of each completed piece overlaps by about 1⁄4", and then carefully clip the thread **(fig. 7).**

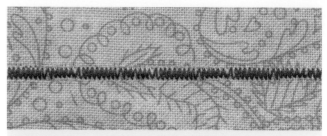

Fig. 5 Set the stitch length and width to sew a satin stitch.

Fig. 6 Satin stitch the outer edges of the appliqué.

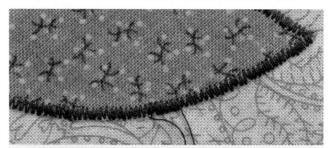

Fig. 7 Overlap the stitches at the starting and stopping points.

• PIN POINT •

Enclosing the Raw Edges

I've learned that the best way to enclose the raw edge of each appliqué is to watch the outer stitch land in the background fabric exactly next to the shape. When the needle swings back toward the inside of the appliqué, the raw edge will automatically be encased in the line of stitches.

"All Fowled Up Embellished Kitchen Towel,"
from Simple Graces

Scrap Basket Blossoms

This scrappy-style four-block quilt combines traditionally designed appliqué elements with simple patchwork, and the result is a project that's perfect for practicing and honing your newfound appliqué skills. Three, two, one— start stitching!

Materials

The fabrics listed below assume a 42" width of usable cotton fabric after prewashing and trimming away the selvages. If you'd prefer to use wool for the appliqués, simply substitute your favorite wool pieces.

- 1⅓ yards of cream print for block backgrounds
- 1 yard of medium-blue print for sashing and border
- Approximately ⅞ yard *total* of assorted print scraps for 16-Patch blocks and binding
- 1 fat quarter (18" x 22") of green stripe or print for stems
- ⅛ yard *each* of dark-red, medium-red, and pink prints for tulip appliqués
- 4" x 15" rectangle *each* of 4 assorted brown and tan prints for vase appliqués
- 1 fat eighth (9" x 22") of medium- or light-blue print for oak-blossom appliqués
- 8" x 8" square of dark-blue print for large oak-blossom center appliqués and berry appliqués
- Scraps of assorted green prints for leaf appliqués
- Scraps of assorted gold prints for small oak-blossom center appliqués
- Scraps of assorted red and pink prints for berry appliqués
- 3¼ yards of fabric for backing
- 58" x 58" square of quilt batting
- Bias bar to fit your stems
- Fabric glue, water-soluble and acid-free
- Supplies for your appliqué method of choice

Designed, pieced, and appliquéd using the invisible machine appliqué method by Kim Diehl; machine quilted by the staff at The Gathering Place, Rupert, Idaho

Finished quilt size: 52½" x 52½" • Finished block size: 20" x 20"

Cutting

Cut all pieces across the width of the fabric in the order given unless otherwise noted. Please refer to the instructions provided in this book for your chosen appliqué method to prepare the appliqués. Refer to "Making Bias-Tube Stems and Vines" (page 18) to cut bias strips. For greater ease, cutting instructions for the tulip appliqués are provided separately. Appliqué patterns A–F are provided on page 61.

From *each* of the dark-red, medium-red, and pink prints, cut:

1 strip, 1¾" x 42"

From the green stripe or print, cut:

4 *bias* strips, 1¼" x 12"

16 *bias* strips, 1¼" x 8"

From the cream print, cut:

4 squares, 20½" x 20½"

From the assorted brown and tan prints, cut a *combined total* of:

4 vases using pattern A

From the medium- or light-blue print for the oak-blossom appliqués, cut:

4 oak blossoms using pattern C

4 reversed oak blossoms using pattern C

From the dark-blue print, cut:

8 large oak-blossom centers using pattern D

Reserve the scraps for the berry appliqués.

From the assorted gold print scraps, cut:

8 small oak-blossom centers in matching sets of 2 using pattern F

From the assorted green print scraps, cut:

56 leaves using pattern D

From the assorted red and pink print scraps and the reserved scraps of dark-blue print, cut a *combined total* of:

72 berries using pattern E

From the assorted print scraps for 16-Patch blocks and binding, cut:

144 squares, 1½" x 1½"

Enough random lengths of 2½"-wide strips to make a 220" length of binding when joined end to end

From the medium-blue print for sashing and border, cut:

6 strips, 4½" x 42"; crosscut into 12 rectangles, 4½" x 20½"

Preparing the Tulip Appliqués

Sew all pieces with right sides together using a ¼" seam allowance unless otherwise noted.

1. Join the dark-red, medium-red, and pink print 1¾" x 42" strips along the long edges to make a strip set, positioning the colors from dark to light. Press the seam allowances toward the pink strip.

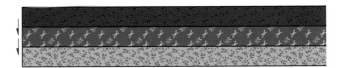

2. Using your chosen method of appliqué, use pattern B to cut and prepare four tulips from the strip set.

Make 4.

Preparing the Stems

Refer to "Making Bias-Tube Stems and Vines" (page 18) to prepare the stems from the 1¼" x 12" and 1¼" x 8" bias strips.

Appliquéing the Blocks

Please refer to the project photo for color placement as you position, baste, and stitch the appliqués using your chosen method of appliqué.

1. Referring to "Preparing to Appliqué" (page 6), prepare each cream 20½" square; see figure 3 of "Crease Styles" (page 7) to include vertical and horizontal creases.

2. Fold a prepared vase appliqué in half, right sides together, and finger-press a center vertical crease.

3. Position the vase appliqué on the prepared background square, with the bottom edge of the vase resting 1¾" up from the bottom raw edge and aligning the center crease with the background crease to perfectly center it from side to side. Pin the vase in place.

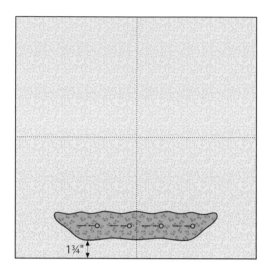

4. Measuring down 1¾" from the top edge of the background square, position a tulip appliqué on the block, with the points resting at the 1¾" position. Align the center of the tulip with the background crease to perfectly center it from side to side. Pin the tulip in place.

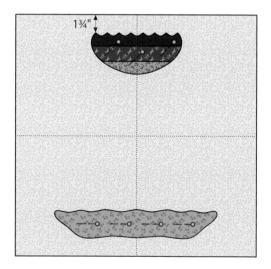

5. Apply small dots of liquid basting glue along the vertical crease between the tulip and vase appliqués. Center a prepared 12" stem over the glue-basted crease and press it in place with your hands, tucking the raw ends under the pinned appliqués.

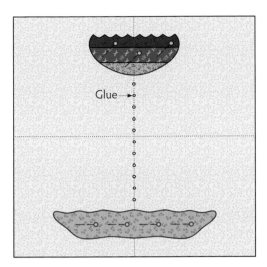

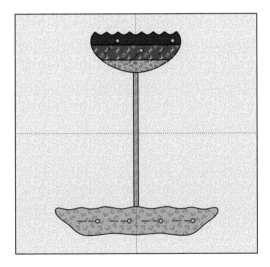

6. Referring to the pictured quilt, position a prepared oak-blossom appliqué onto the right-hand side of the background square. (This will give you something to aim for when you lay out your stem.)

7. Apply small dots of liquid basting glue to the seam allowance of a prepared 8" stem. Referring to the quilt photo, position the prepared stem onto the right-hand side of the background square, placing the bottom edge approximately 1" above the horizontal background crease. Tuck the raw end of the 8" stem under the main stem (trimming away any corner portion that may be visible after you establish the angle of the curve) and position it to meet the oak blossom. Tuck the tip of the stem under the oak blossom, ensuring the pieces overlap by approximately ¼". Trim away any excess stem length.

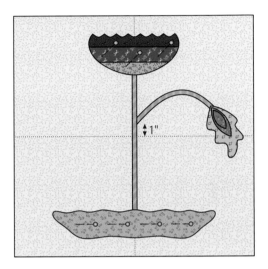

8. In the same manner, apply basting glue to a second 8" stem and position it onto the right-hand side of the background square, measuring up approximately 2" from the top of the vase appliqué to the bottom edge of the stem, and duplicating the curve established when laying out the first 8" stem.

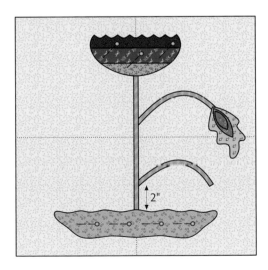

9. Repeat steps 6–8 to glue baste and position two additional prepared 8" stems onto the left-hand side of the background, placing them in mirror images to the stems on the right-hand side of the block.

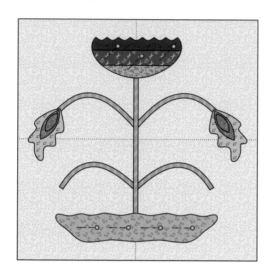

10. Referring to the pictured quilt, lay out the leaves prepared from the assorted green print scraps. When you're pleased with the arrangement, baste the leaves in place.

11. Remove the tulip, vase, and oak blossom appliqués. Use your chosen method of appliqué to stitch the stems and leaves to the background. If your appliqué method includes freezer paper, remember to remove the pattern pieces from the stitched shapes as instructed in "Removing Paper Pattern Pieces" (page 26).

12. Reposition, baste, and stitch the tulip, vase, and oak blossom appliqués. If applicable, remove the freezer-paper pattern pieces. Continue working from the bottom layer to the top to add the remaining appliqués, removing any freezer-paper pattern pieces after each layer has been stitched.

13. Repeat steps 1–12 to make a total of four appliquéd blocks measuring 20½" square, including the seam allowances.

Piecing and Adding the Borders

1. Join the assorted print 1½" squares in sets of two to make 72 pairs.

Make 72.

2. Join the pairs from step 1 in sets of two to make 36 row units consisting of four squares each. Press the seam allowances of each unit in one direction.

Make 36.

3. Lay out four units from step 1 to make a 16-Patch block, alternating the direction of the pressed seam allowances with every other row so the seams nest together. Join the rows. Press the seam allowances in one direction. Repeat for a total of nine 16-Patch blocks measuring 4½" square, including the seam allowances.

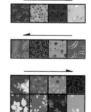

Make 9.

4. Lay out three 16-Patch blocks and two medium-blue 4½" x 20½" rectangles in alternating positions to form a row. Join the pieces. Press the seam allowances toward the medium-blue print. Repeat for a total of three pieced sashing rows.

5. Lay out three medium-blue print 4½" x 20½" rectangles and two appliquéd blocks in alternating positions. Join the pieces. Carefully press the seam allowances toward the medium-blue print, taking care not to apply heat to the appliqués. Repeat for a total of two pieced block rows.

6. Referring to the pictured quilt, lay out three pieced sashing rows and two pieced block rows to form the quilt top. Join the rows. Carefully press the seam allowances toward the sashing rows. The pieced quilt top should now measure 52½" square, including the seam allowances.

Completing the Quilt

Layer the quilt top, batting, and backing. Quilt the layers. For Kim's quilt, the background areas of the blocks were machine quilted with a McTavishing design (free-form shapes that are echo quilted inward) to frame the appliqués. Stitched accents were added to the larger appliqué shapes to enhance them. The sashing and border strips were quilted with feathered sprays, and the border background areas were filled in with a tiny stipple design. For a traditional feel, Xs were stitched through the squares of the checkerboard units. Join the random lengths of assorted print 2½"-wide strips to make a 220"-long pieced strip and use it to bind the quilt.

One-Block Wall Hanging

Making one block is a great way to try out a new appliqué technique and gain a beautiful wall hanging without investing a lot of time and supplies.

Finished quilt size: 28½" x 28½" • Finished block size: 20" x 20"

Materials

The fabrics listed below assume a 42" width of usable cotton fabric after prewashing and trimming away the selvages. If you'd prefer to use wool for the appliqués, simply substitute your favorite wool pieces.

- ⅔ yard of cream print for block background
- Approximately ½ yard *total* of assorted print scraps for 16-Patch blocks and binding
- ⅓ yard of medium-blue print for border
- 1 fat eighth (9" x 22") of medium-green stripe or print for stems
- 1 fat eighth of medium-brown print for vase appliqué
- 1 chubby sixteenth (9" x 11") of medium- or light-blue print for oak blossom appliqués
- 1 chubby sixteenth of dark-blue print for large oak-blossom center and berry appliqués
- 1¾" x 10" strip *each* of red, dark-pink, and medium-pink prints for tulip appliqué

- 5" x 5" square of gold print for small oak-blossom center appliqués
- Scraps of assorted green prints for leaf appliqués
- Scraps of assorted red and pink prints for berry appliqués
- 1⅛ yards of fabric for backing
- 36" x 36" square of quilt batting
- Bias bar to fit your stems
- Fabric glue, water-soluble and acid-free
- Supplies for your appliqué method of choice

Cutting

Cut all pieces across the width of the fabric in the order given unless otherwise noted. Please refer to the instructions provided in this book for your chosen appliqué method to prepare the appliqués. Refer to "Making Bias-Tube Stems and Vines" (page 18) to cut bias strips. For greater ease, cutting instructions for the tulip appliqués are provided separately. Appliqué patterns A–F are provided on page 61.

From the *bias** of the medium-green stripe or print, cut:

1 strip, 1¼" x 12"
4 strips, 1¼" x 8"
* It isn't necessary to cut the above strips using a true 45° bias angle; cut them at an angle that will best accommodate the size of your fat eighth, and this will result in enough "give" to the stems to allow them to curve as you lay out the stem design.

From the cream print, cut:

1 square, 20½" x 20½"

From the medium-brown print, cut:

1 vase using pattern A

From the medium- or light-blue print, cut:

1 oak blossom using pattern C
1 reversed oak blossom using pattern C

From the dark-blue print, cut:

2 large oak-blossom centers using pattern D
Reserve the scraps for the berry appliqués.

From the gold print, cut:

2 small oak-blossom centers using pattern F

From the assorted green print scraps, cut:

14 leaves using pattern D

From the assorted red and pink print scraps and the reserved scraps of dark-blue print, cut a *combined total* of:

18 berries using pattern E

From the assorted print scraps, cut:

64 squares, 1½" x 1½"
Enough random lengths of 2½"-wide strips to make a 124" length of binding when joined end to end

From the medium-blue print designated for the border, cut:

4 strips, 4½" x 20½"

Assembling the Wall Hanging

Sew all pieces with right sides together using a ¼" seam allowance unless otherwise noted.

1. Refer to the instructions for "Scrap Basket Blossoms" (page 53) to make one appliquéd block and four 16-Patch blocks.

2. Sew a medium-blue 4½" x 20½" border strip to the sides of the appliquéd block. Carefully press the seam allowances toward the borders, taking care not to apply heat to the appliqués. Add a 16-Patch block to the ends of the remaining two medium-blue border strips. Press the seam allowances toward the strips. Join the pieced strips to the top and bottom of the appliquéd block. Carefully press the seam allowances toward the pieced borders. The quilt top should now measure 28½" square, including the seam allowances.

3. Layer the quilt top, batting, and backing. Quilt the layers. Join the random lengths of assorted print 2½"-wide strips to make a 124"-long pieced strip and use it to bind the quilt.

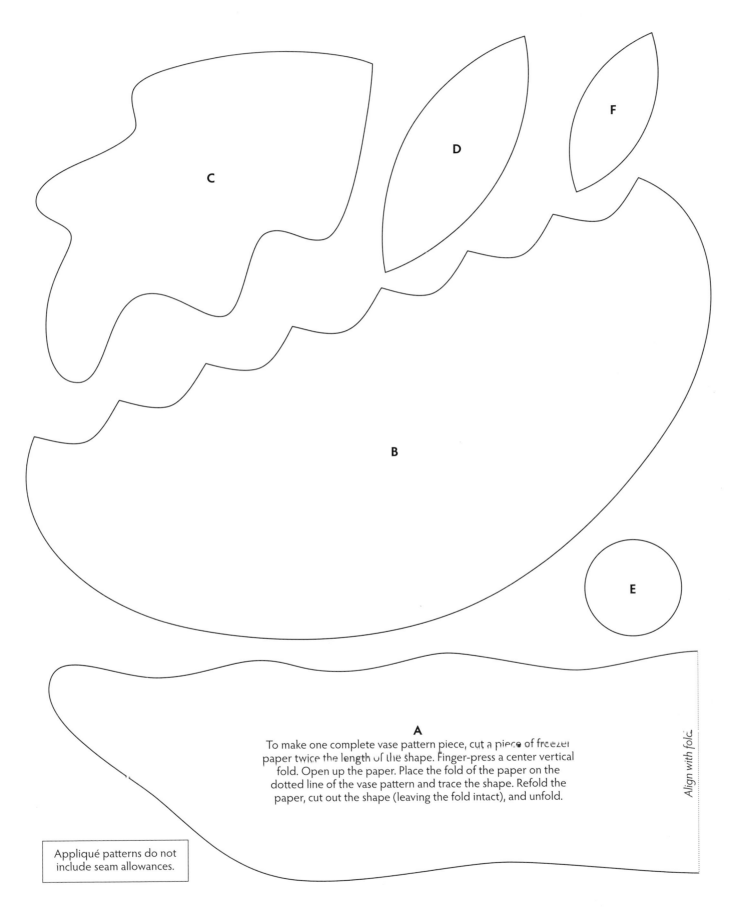

C

D

F

B

E

A

To make one complete vase pattern piece, cut a piece of freezer paper twice the length of the shape. Finger-press a center vertical fold. Open up the paper. Place the fold of the paper on the dotted line of the vase pattern and trace the shape. Refold the paper, cut out the shape (leaving the fold intact), and unfold.

Align with fold

Appliqué patterns do not include seam allowances.

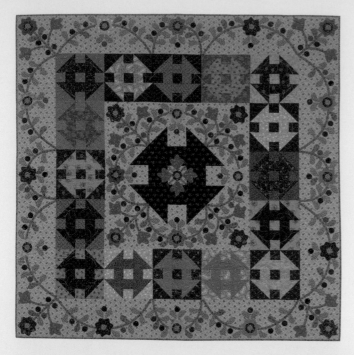

About the Author

After teaching herself the steps needed to make a quilt in the late 1990's, Kim entered and won *American Patchwork & Quilting* magazine's "Pieces of the Past" quilt challenge with just the third quilt she'd ever made, sending her life down a new and unexpected path. Winning this national challenge led to publishing quilts in magazines, which led to her best-selling series of "Simple" books with Martingale, and ultimately to traveling around the country and teaching workshops featuring her easy appliqué methods.

Kim's very favorite quilts have always been those sewn from simple tried-and-true patchwork designs, especially when combined with appliqué, and she loves designing and stitching her quilts using modern techniques for a perfect blend of tradition and convenience.

In addition to designing quilts, teaching her appliqué methods, and writing quilting books, Kim designs fabric lines for Henry Glass & Co., including her "Simple Whatnots Club" project collections.

What an unexpected blessing to discover a hobby that she feels so passionately about, and then watch it blossom into a full-time career!

Also by Kim Diehl

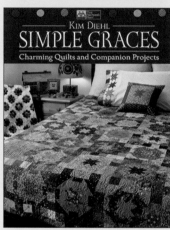

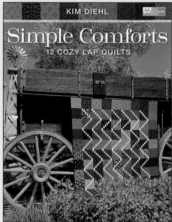

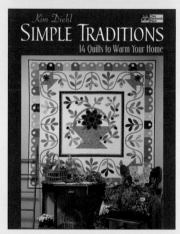

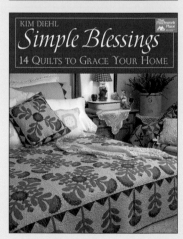